EASTER

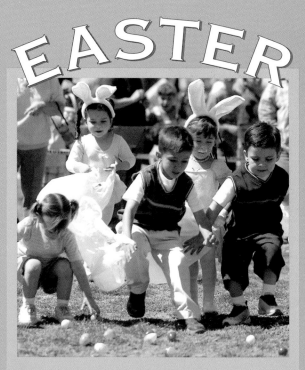

A TRUE BOOK®

by
Nancy I. Sanders

Children's Press®
A Division of Scholastic Inc.

New York Toronto London Auckland Sydney
Mexico City New Delhi Hong Kong
Danbury, Connecticut

Ukrainian dancers
at New York City's
Easter Parade

Reading Consultant
Jeanne Clidas, Ph.D.
*National Reading Consultant
and Professor of Reading,
SUNY Brockport*

Dedication
*For Danny and our happy
Easter memories.*

Library of Congress Cataloging-in-Publication Data

Sanders, Nancy I.
    Easter / by Nancy I. Sanders.— 1st American ed.
        p. cm.—(A true book)
    Includes bibliographical references and index.
Contents: A celebration of joy—Death and resurrection — Ancient Spring
celebrations — Different customs in different countries — Let's celebrate!
ISBN 0-516-22763-7 (lib. bdg.)   0-516-27777-4 (pbk.)
    1. Easter—Juvenile literature. [1. Easter. 2. Jesus Christ—Resurrection.
3. Holidays.] I. Title. II. Series.
GT4935.S235 2003
394.2667—dc21

                                              2003004522

Contents

A Celebration of Joy

Spring is a time to celebrate. The days are getting warmer. Flowers are blooming. Baby animals are born.

Spring is also the season during which people celebrate Easter. For many people, Easter is a happy festival that celebrates new life. For **Christians,**

A church service
on Easter Sunday

Easter is the most important holiday of the year. It celebrates the Resurrection of Jesus Christ—the day he rose from the dead.

Easter occurs in either March or April. Though the exact date of Easter changes from year to year, it always comes on a Sunday, to honor the day of Jesus' resurrection. It is always celebrated on the first Sunday after the full moon following the spring **equinox**.

Death and Resurrection

The New Testament of the Bible tells of how about two thousand years ago, a Jewish carpenter named Jesus lived in the land known today as Israel. Jesus taught his followers about God. Many people believed Jesus was the son of God.

A painting showing Jesus teaching his followers

Jesus and his followers celebrated Passover, the spring festival of freedom for Jewish people. During this holiday, Jews remembered how their ancestors became free after being slaves in Egypt.

Jesus and his followers went to Jerusalem for the Passover holiday. Jesus rode into this holy city on a donkey as a symbol of peace. By this point, he was famous. Men, women, and children cheered for him. They waved palm branches to honor him.

Later that week, Jesus ate a special meal with his closest

People waved palm branches to honor Jesus as he entered Jerusalem.

This painting shows Jesus pointing to the bread and the wine during the Last Supper. The ritual of sharing bread and wine to remember Jesus' body and blood is called Communion. Christians still practice this ritual today.

followers. These twelve men were called his **disciples**. Their final meal together has become known as the Last Supper.

At the Last Supper, Jesus commanded his followers to remember him after his death. He gave them bread. This would remind them of his body. He gave them wine. This would remind them of his blood. Jesus taught that his body and his blood would be an important **sacrifice** to make up for people's sins—the wrong things they had done.

After the meal was over, Jesus and his disciples walked to a place called the Garden of Gethsemane. Some of the Jewish leaders disagreed with Jesus' teachings. Judas, one of Jesus' disciples, brought these leaders to the garden. Roman soldiers were with them. They arrested Jesus and led him away.

A painting showing Roman soldiers arresting Jesus

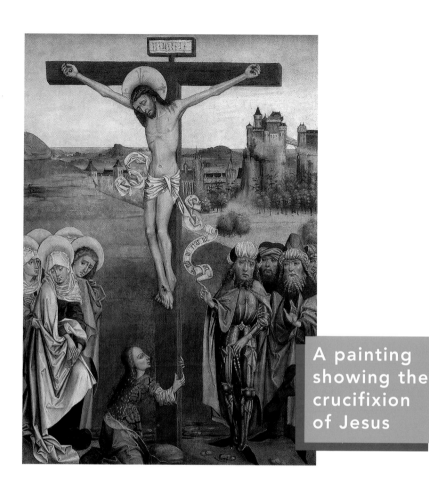

Jesus was put on **trial**. He was beaten. He was sentenced to the Roman punishment of death by crucifixion—hanging on a cross. After Jesus died, his followers were very sad. They put his body in a **tomb**.

On the following Sunday, however, an amazing thing happened. Jesus' friends looked in the tomb, but it was empty. Jesus suddenly appeared and spoke to his friends. He had risen from the dead. This is called the Resurrection.

Excitement spread quickly among his followers. They met often with Jesus. He

On the Sunday after he died, Jesus rose from the dead.

encouraged them to tell others the news. Jesus visited with his friends for forty days until he went up to heaven.

Forty days after
Jesus rose from
the dead, he rose
to heaven.

His followers watched him
ascend, or rise, into the sky. He
disappeared in the clouds. Today
this is called the Ascension.

Days Leading up to Easter

Ash Wednesday This day marks the beginning of Lent, the season of prayer and **fasting** before Easter. On this day, ashes in the shape of a cross are put on people's foreheads as a sign of their sorrow for their sins.

Palm Sunday This is the Sunday before Easter. On this day, palm branches are carried in memory of the crowds that honored Jesus when he entered Jerusalem.

Holy Thursday On this day, Christians share bread and wine to remember the commands Jesus gave at the Last Supper.

Good Friday This is the day set aside to honor Jesus' death.

Ancient Spring Celebrations

Easter has a very long history.
Many years before Jesus lived,
people living in northern
Europe celebrated the coming
of spring. At that time, many
believed that a goddess
named Eostre brought spring
to the land. This name may be

People have celebrated the coming of spring for thousands of years.

where the word "Easter" comes from.

Springtime festivals were held. People lit fires outdoors. They put on clean or new clothes. They danced and sang for joy.

It is an ancient European tradition to give gifts of eggs in the spring.

Everyone was happy that the cold days of winter were ending. They gave gifts of eggs to each other. Eggs were a symbol that life would begin again.

After the death and Resurrection of Jesus, Christians had
a new holiday to celebrate.
Because this had happened
during the spring festival of
Passover, Christians began to
celebrate their new holiday
each year in the spring. Often,
springtime festivals and the
new Christian holiday were
celebrated side by side. Over
the years, traditions from
springtime festivals became a
part of the Christian holiday.

Symbols of Easter

Symbol	Meaning
Bells	Rung to call people to rejoice
Bread and grape juice or wine	Symbols of Jesus' body and blood
Candles	The promise of light after darkness
Cross	Reminder of the death of Jesus

◀ Church bells

▼ Bread and wine for communion

◀ Easter candle

▶ A cross covered with Easter lilies

Symbol	Meaning
Eggs	Sign of spring and new life
Flowers	Hope of new life
Lamb	Symbol of the sacrifice Jesus made by his death
Palm branches	Waved to honor Jesus on Palm Sunday, the day he rode into Jerusalem
Rabbits	Sign of new life

◄ Easter eggs

▼ Painting of the "Lamb of God"

► Altar boys carrying palms on Palm Sunday

► Chocolate rabbits

Let's Celebrate!

Millions of people across the United States celebrate Easter. To prepare for the holiday, many people buy new outfits to wear.

Children also enjoy decorating eggs. They may dye them with food coloring or decorate them with stickers or glitter.

Many families dress up in new outfits for Easter (left). Some children like to color eggs for Easter (above).

Some people create pretty designs by wrapping eggs in onion skins before dipping them into boiling solutions of dye.

A girl holding an Easter basket

Many children wake up on Easter morning filled with excitement. They think a special rabbit called the Easter Bunny visited their homes while they were sleeping. They look for special baskets he might have left behind. Will their baskets contain chocolate bunnies, candy eggs, and jelly beans this year?

Some people go to church on Easter morning. They sing beautiful **hymns** and songs. They tell each other, "Jesus has risen!" For Christians, Easter is the most joyous holiday of the year.

Children participating in an Easter Sunday church service

A family gathered around the table for Easter dinner

Families often gather for a special dinner. It is a tradition to serve ham or lamb on Easter. After the meal, the children may take part in an egg hunt. The parents may have hidden the hard-boiled eggs the children dyed or colored. Some families hunt for plastic eggs with candy or small toys hidden inside.

Some famous special events are held on Easter. New York City is known for its Easter

Parade. People stroll down Fifth Avenue wearing fancy hats. Sometimes **celebrities** join in the fun. Onlookers keep their cameras ready and take lots of pictures.

For more than one hundred years, Washington, D.C., has been the site of a very special Easter tradition. On Easter Monday when the weather is good, an egg-rolling contest for young children is held on the White House lawn. Often,

Two famous Easter events are New York City's Easter Parade (left) and the egg-rolling contest on the White House lawn in Washington, D.C. (below).

The Easter sunrise service at the Hollywood Bowl in Los Angeles

the president of the United States and his wife, the first lady, are there to greet the young visitors.

One of the nation's most famous Easter services is held at the Hollywood Bowl in California. More than thirty thousand people gather early Sunday morning. They watch the sunrise at this outdoor theater. Various church groups and community groups sing beautiful hymns and perform special Easter music.

Easter Customs Around the World

Easter is celebrated in various ways throughout the world. In Spain and many Latin American countries, magnificent parades are held during Holy Week, the week before Easter. The most important parades of all are held on Good Friday. Fancy

A Holy Week procession in El Salvador

floats pass down the streets, carrying statues of Jesus and his mother, Mary. Penitents, people who feel sorry for their sins, walk slowly along with the floats.

People lighting candles
in Russia on Easter Eve

In many countries throughout Eastern Europe, people
light candles in their homes

and churches on the night before Easter, called Easter Eve. These candles are lit as a symbol of how Jesus rose from the dead to bring light to the world.

In Greece, fireworks light up the streets on Easter Eve. People shout for joy. It is a happy and exciting time.

Samiland is an area covering parts of northern Finland, Norway, Sweden, and Russia. The Sami people

The start of an Easter
reindeer race in Samiland

live throughout this area. Many
Sami raise reindeer for a living.
To celebrate Easter, the Sami
hold festivals with exciting
events such as reindeer racing.

In several eastern European countries, including Hungary, Poland, and Ukraine, it is an Easter tradition to paint eggs with colorful, **intricate** patterns.

Children painting Ukrainian Easter eggs

Some of these designs have been handed down from one generation to the next.

Whether people celebrate Easter because of their Christian **beliefs**, the arrival of spring, or both, it is a favorite holiday for many. New life and new beginnings make everyone feel happy. They look forward to springtime and the brighter days ahead.

To Find Out More

Here are some additional resources to help you learn more about Easter:

 **Books**

Barth, Edna. **Lilies, Rabbits, and Painted Eggs.** Clarion, 1998.

Chambers, Catherine. **Easter.** (A World of Holidays). Raintree/ Steck Vaughn, 1998.

Fisher, Aileen. **The Story of Easter.** Harper Trophy, 1998.

Greenfield, Eloise. **Easter Parade.** Disney Press, 1998.

Kalman, Bobbie. **We Celebrate Easter.** Crabtree, 1985.

O'Neal, Debbie Trafton. **Before and After Easter: Activities and Ideas for Lent to Pentecost.** Augsburg Fortress, 2001.

Organizations and Online Sites

Absolutely Easter
*http://www.geocities.com/
Heartland/7134/Easter/*

Not only can you learn
about chocolate, rabbits,
and the meaning of Easter
on this website, but you
can also print out and
assemble an Easter village,
complete with buildings,
rabbits, and a landscape.

Easter Celebrations from
The Holiday Spot
*http://www.theholidayspot.
com/easter/*

Easter music plays while
you hunt on this site for
recipes such as carrot cake
and Easter-basket cup-
cakes. Crafts, stories,
Easter cards, and party
ideas are included, along
with some special Easter
fonts for your computer.

Easter on the Net
*http://www.holidays.net/
easter/*

Learn all about Easter: its
history, symbols, dates, and
more. There are movies to
download, crafts to make,
pictures to color, and a
message board on which
to share your own favorite
traditions.

How to Make Ukrainian
Easter Eggs
*http://www.ns.sympatico.
ca/amorash/main.html*

Learn how to make beauti-
ful eggs with Ukrainian
designs. An explanation of
the colors and symbols
used is included. Adult
supervision is required for
making these eggs.

Important Words

beliefs ideas people hold to be true

celebrities famous people

Christians people who follow the teachings of Jesus Christ

disciples twelve men who were the closest followers of Jesus

equinox day of the year when the sun crosses the equator, so that the day and the night are of equal length

fasting going without food for a period of time

hymns songs of praise, especially to God

intricate complicated or detailed

sacrifice to give up something valuable to help others

tomb place used to bury the dead

trial examination and judgment of a person by a lawmaking group

Index

Meet the Author

When Nancy I. Sanders was a girl, her favorite thing to do was to read books. *Winnie-the-Pooh, Ramona the Pest,* and *My Friend Flicka* were some of her favorites. Nancy still loves to read, but now one of things she enjoys doing is writing.

She has authored many books, including craft books, easy readers, nonfiction books, Bible stories, and books for teachers.

Nancy and her husband, Jeff, like to visit places with their sons, Dan and Ben. They've toured Yosemite, photographed bison in Yellowstone, and stood on top of the Empire State Building. Nancy and her family live in Chino, California.